Sunflower Garden

LEARN WREATH DESIGN

NANCY ALEXANDER

By World-Renowned
Floral Designer – Nancy Alexander

Ladybug wreaths

Want to Watch a Free Wreath Tip Video from Nancy?

Go To: **www.LadybugWreaths.com/sg**

Publisher's Disclaimer

No part of this book may be duplicated, stored in an information retrieval system, or sent in any form or by any available resource, electronic, mechanical, photographic reproduction, recorded material, scanning, optically, either digital or analog or otherwise, except as permitted under Section 107 or 108 of the 1976 United States Copyright Act, without the prior written permission of the Publisher or Author.

Requests to the Author or Publisher for permission should be addressed to:
Ladybug Wreaths
203 Regent Road
Anderson, SC 29621

Limit of Liability/Disclaimer of Warranty: While the publisher and the author have used their best abilities in assembling this book, they make no representations or warranties with respect to the exactness or wholeness of the contents of this book and particularly reject any implied warranties of marketability or appropriateness for a particular purpose. No warranty may be developed or continued by sales representatives or written sales materials.

The information and methods contained herein may not be useful for your circumstances. The reader should confer with a professional where suitable. Neither the publisher nor the author shall be responsible for any loss of profit or any other commercial injuries, including but not limited to special, incidental, significant, or other damages.

If you would like to begin receiving our popular and Free newsletter with valuable information, visit: http://www.LadybugWreaths.com. We would love to add you to our subscriber list.

Please email nancy@LadybugWreaths.com to report illegal distribution.

As of the writing of this book, all information is current. Please note that over time, this type of information may change – especially when writing and picturing seasonal items.

CONTENTS

ABOUT THE AUTHOR

Nancy Alexander is a wife, mother, Mimi, sister, best friend, and child of God.

As a Dreamer, Artisan, Teacher, Public Speaker, Coach and Internet Entrepreneur, it didn't take long for her to become known as a world-renowned Floral and Interior Designer.

After over 30 years of running her own businesses, she now sells popular floral designs, as well as her how-to, instructional DVDs and downloadable videos.

But, that's not all! Nancy is a published author offering several popular Books. Her life story is being written with a published author.

Nancy is blessed to know, work, and partner with many of the most talented "Internet Entrepreneurs" in the business.

Nancy **LOVES** her students, as she shares in their joy and excitement with every accomplishment!

"Nancy's dreams are to make YOUR dreams come true by equipping and teaching YOU to become a success!" You'll quite often hear Nancy's encouraging words saying "You Can Do It!...I Know YOU Can!"

In the last 10 years well over 3,000 wreaths have been shipped to happy customers all over the world. She has sold thousands of videos and e-books which teach her customers how to design and sell their own floral creations!

Nancy, and her best friend and partner, Linda Joseph, offer private and group coaching. This one-on-one or group coaching has made a huge

difference in many lives. You can find more information about these coaching venues on their latest website:
www.PassionIntoProfits.com

Their coaching/membership site, **www.BestOfNancy.com** encourages and trains women to develop their "artisan" skills as they learn to sell and promote crafts and products online through many venues.

Another Ladybug Wreath's site, **www.LadybugCertified.com** provides the exact same supplies Nancy uses in all her wreaths. Available from Amazon, shipping is FREE with Amazon Prime. Benefits are…no Sales Tax ID is required; no case quantities; no minimums; and super-fast shipping.

Group & Private (VIP) workshops offered in her home studio are such fun. After experiencing a "Studio Day" with Nancy, each lady departs with a gorgeous wreath and an easel. They possess the tools to start a budding business or to make gorgeous wreaths as a hobby.

Nancy says: "I am thrilled to know these ladies are leaving with confidence and knowledge to set up online and offline businesses to sell their beautiful creations. But, most importantly, I am also filled with JOY as they leave with hugs, laughter, and lots of smiles."

Nancy has been encouraged, and coached by her mentor and dear friend, Jim Cockrum. Nancy admires Jim and calls him one of the most ethical Internet Marketers around, and all the while Jim says *"Nancy has inspired me* more than I could *ever* inspire her." As a matter of fact, Jim has written about Nancy in his newly published book; **"FREE Marketing 101"**. This book is **the number one** book on Internet Marketing in the world!

Nancy is inundated with emails and calls from her faithful followers who want and need her to help them. You see, Nancy has been fighting a painful battle with Fibromyalgia and Celiac Disease after becoming severely ill at twenty-eight years of age. Thanks to her husband, Steve, amazing doctors and God's leading; she is enjoying a new life!

Nancy has a heart-felt yearning to help others regain their health, & experience positive changes as she has. She desires for each of you to find joy, health, and happiness through God's leading and through your own successful business. This has turned into quite a ministry for Nancy and Steve.

INTRODUCTION

Welcome and Congratulations on your purchase of Sunflower Garden Wreath Instructional Book!

Wreath making can become one of the easiest and most delightful hobbies you will ever undertake. I taught myself how to make a wreath many, many years ago during a difficult time in my life. I was struggling to feel normal while experiencing chronic pain, so wreath making became an outlet of self-expression and creativity. I first sold my wreaths at craft shows, and after finding success there, I purchased a local shop called The Straw Basket. This purchase was a highlight in my life, allowing me to develop my own style in floral design. The business grew, taking me down several avenues, which eventually led me to eBay. I didn't stop there! I now sell wreaths to faithful customers all over the world, while other parts of my business continue to grow by leaps and bounds.

For many years I have received requests from friends, customers, and new acquaintances alike wanting to learn my style in designing one-of-a-kind wreaths. Customers and friends in my hometown tell me when they visit a home or doctor's office in town; they always recognize my wreaths and my style immediately. Well, this book is geared to instruct, but most of all to help you develop your own style, which has been and will always be my goal!

I have poured hours of labor and creativity into Sunflower Garden so that you can learn the basics -- each step in building (and yes, it is a building process) your own wreath. **I will be sharing with you some of my tips and secrets for making gorgeous wreaths.** I encourage you to follow along closely and then add your own creative touch.

These quality tips and secrets will help you make your very own wreath that can withstand the weather, birds looking for a place to nest, and the occasional fall from your door. If you begin each wreath or design in the right way by tightly securing each stem, bloom, bird, birdhouse, nest, etc., then your wreath will hold up for many, many years. Sun damage, which, unfortunately, is inevitable, may occur, even with quality materials.

You will also learn how to make your wreath "wild & woodsy", "light & airy", or very full and formal.

These phrases have described my personal style, but in the long run, and with lots of practice, you will eventually start to see your own style developing. This style will be exclusive to you, your likes and dislikes, and will reflect the unique and special person that you are. _I can guarantee that it will be absolutely beautiful!!_

Sunflower Garden also includes a list of suggested supplies, in addition to a list of the particular items I used for the wreath on the cover. Please go to your local craft/floral store to purchase the stems that best suit your style and taste, or visit my supplies store: **www.LadybugCertified.com**. Always remember, available supplies change from year to year. You may not be able to purchase exactly what I used here. Just find something as close as you can.

I offer several books as well as instructional DVDs and digital videos and wreath design. You can learn more in the **Resource Appendix**.

ITEMS YOU WILL NEED

Wreath Making Tools

- **Glue gun and glue sticks***
- **Wire cutters***
- **Floral tape**
- **Picks**
- **Pipe Cleaners**
- **Easel (optional)***

  ***NOTE:** I use a custom made easel which you can purchase here: http://ladybugwreaths.com/doorwreaths/product/wreath-making-supplies/

Supplies for the Sunflower Garden Wreath

(Supplies can be found at LadybugCertified.com, your local craft store or Wholesale Supplier.)

- **Wild birch wreath – large or small***
- **Section of freshly harvested honeysuckle vine**
- **Green ficus leaf stem**
- **Ivy bunch**
- **Green grasses**
- **Three large sunflowers**
- **Seven tearose Gerber daisies**
- **Two different berry stems, whatever you can find**
- **Tiny deep purple berry cluster stems**
- **Airy yellow filler**
- **Yellow spikey filler**
- **Tearose Verbena**
- **Two birds, bumblebees, ladybug**
- **Miscellaneous fruit in a mixture of colors**
- **Sponge mushroom stems**
- **Several different types of greenery including a bunch of ivy, grasses (short, long) & airy leafy stem**

MAKING YOUR WREATH

CHAPTER 1 – LET'S MAKE A WREATH

The wreath I used is one of our custom-made wild birch wreaths. A young mother, who lives in the hills of Kentucky, makes them exclusively for Ladybug Wreaths and personally drives 9 hours each way to bring them to me.

These custom made wreaths are available for purchase through our new Amazon store: www.LadybugCertified.com Also, all wreaths that I design for you are made from these same Wild Birch wreaths.

CHAPTER 2 – PREPARING YOUR WREATH

Place the wreath on your easel or door until it hangs evenly to find a top and a bottom. You'll know when you find the right spot. I want the wild birch stems to point up, and down. This makes it look more like an oval wreath before you even begin.

If you would like to create a more "wild and woodsy" look, cut off "curly" stems from your honeysuckle vine and glue them into the outside of the wreath. The sticks along with honeysuckle vine radiating and curling out will give your wreath a look just like mine.

Let's put a wreath hanger on the back of our wreath before we do anything else. Begin by picking up one of your pipe cleaners. Work from the back of the wreath, tying the pipe cleaner to one of the heavier portions of your wreath exactly on the top.

Making sure you attach it to one of the thicker, sturdier stems in the wreath assures that no matter how much weight you add, you know that your wreath will always hang securely even when a door may open and close many times during the day. We don't want it to fall off the door now do we?

Tie the chenille stem and leave yourself a loop at the top to hang it from a door hanger or a nail.

The wreath you see on our cover and at the end of this book is the wreath that was designed to be the "star" of this wreath course. Its base is a "wild birch wreath" which I use exclusively as the base of every wreath I design.

CHAPTER 3 – GOTTA HAVE WILD HONEYSUCKLE

Have you searched for your wild honeysuckle yet? It grows wild in trees, on the side of the road, in the woods, etc. It is easy to find if you look for it and will add such a natural feel to your wreath! Make sure you look around in the springtime when it is in full bloom with its beautiful yellow blossoms. Then, remember where you saw it so you can go back and harvest it anytime you may need it. Finding the colorful, yellow blooms makes it very easy for you to spot it from the side of the road or in the woods behind your home, etc.

When you're ready to harvest some, take some garden clippers with you and cut it at the bottom. It is usually growing up the tree, so all you have to do is start pulling it down. Now, you might have to take someone with you with a little strength. We have been able to pull a lot of ours down ourselves. Be careful! One day, I pulled too hard, and ended up on my bottom on the side of the road! Ha Ha

I personally like the white look of some of the stems rather that the dark stems. The white just seem to stand out more against my birch wreaths and the variation really looks great. I don't just use the fatter stems, but use the smaller ones, sometimes clumped together, also.

Next take the fresh honeysuckle that you picked to make the wild loops and curls in your wreath. I add anywhere from 2 to 8 feet in each wreath, depending on how it looks.

The loops and curls add so much depth and wildness to a wreath – sort of like a three-dimensional look.

Adding honeysuckle is so much fun, and so easy! Before any of the honeysuckle is cut, insert one end into your wreath and out the back about ½ to 1 inch.

Sometimes, it wants to curl in its own direction rather than the way I might want it to go – so I let it. It comes out natural and interesting every single time.

At this point you can cut off the excess from the back of your wreath. Secure it to a branch using one half of a pipe cleaner. Apply hot glue to your stem on the front and back just to make sure it doesn't slip out.

Remember, do not cut your honeysuckle, but instead work with the long piece. You'll find fresh honeysuckle works in small and large wreaths alike.

Sun exposure or age can cause breakage in vines as they dry out, so keep yours as fresh as possible. You can then bend and twist it as you wish. I start by looping my vine out and around the bottom of my wreath.

Don't worry if the honeysuckle sticks out up to 6 to 8 inches. Depending on how large your wreath is, it will only add depth and character to your wreath. **THE WILDER, THE BETTER...I always say!**

Follow along the natural lines of the wreath, securing your vine where it naturally bends back towards the wreath. Stick the end of the honeysuckle into the actual loops of your wreath pulling it out the other side. Or, if you have a loose branch sticking out a little from the others, you can wrap your honeysuckle around it a couple of times.

All of this makes honeysuckle fit more securely, assuring you that it won't come loose. Then, as a final measure, I always make sure to tie it securely with a pipe cleaner.

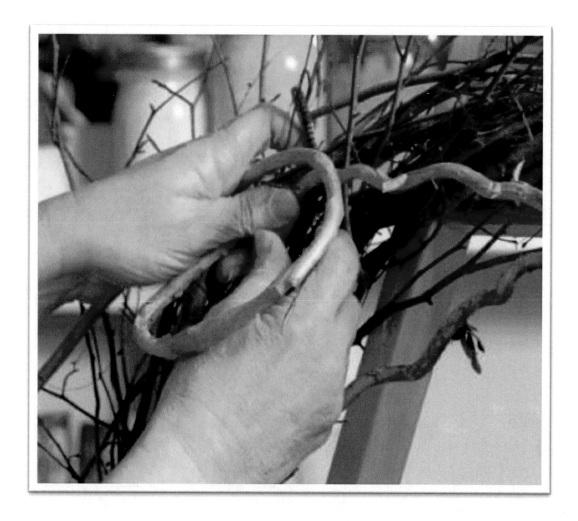

Continue moving the vine up and around the wreath while twisting it into loops and curls. Try making a complete circle as you see me doing in this picture. Make sure you tie that circle securely with a pipe cleaner, and then add moss and glue for a more natural look.

This circle would create a perfect spot for a bird's nest, a perched bird, or a preserved mushroom. You can insert a small mushroom underneath the loop; add moss and fashion your own nest with a very sweet bird perched inside! Be creative when forming these loops and curls of fresh honeysuckle.

Don't be afraid to let it stick out really far, and loop down really low! You want it to look wild! In this picture, I have a pretty large loop hanging down on the left side! Neat, huh?

Then when you add the glue and moss to cover your pipe cleaners, the joints in your wreath already are starting to take on that woodsy look.

In the picture above I am adding some extra pictures of this step. I really want you to see how vital honeysuckle is to the foundation of my wild & woodsy wreaths.

We don't want it to be perfectly symmetrical, so please don't try to make each side the same with loops opposite each other. All of your loops and curls need to be random. Remember, you can never add too much, so, if you like this like me...be generous.

Remember that honeysuckle is much easier to work with, and to bend into these tight loops and curls, when it is very fresh. It will stay fresh for a while, depending on temperature and weather conditions, but then it starts getting brittle and will break easily when you bend it.

In order to prevent glue drips, have a small pinch of moss ready to stick in on top of the hot glue before it runs out and down your wreath. By putting a little moss on each pipe cleaner, pick or stem that shows from the front, you will make the wreath look fuller and more professional because it will hide the "tools of your trade", i.e., the picks, glue, etc.

Moss is often the small touch that ties an entire wreath together. It may seem insignificant right now, but as your wreath unfolds, adding moss will fill gaps, add texture and make your wreath look more natural and "woodsy". In this picture, this wreath is already taking on the "wild & woodsy" look I love so much.   I hope you love it, too!

The spot in this picture covered with moss already looks like a little bird has been working away building her nest!

In the next picture you can see a completed version of my wreath after all the honeysuckle's loops and curls have been added.

You can also see where the moss is hiding all of the pipe cleaners that were used in this process. I really love the way the wreath looks at this point!

Sometimes I'm just tempted to leave it with the moss, honeysuckle, a few greens, and sponge mushrooms. Oh yes, and maybe just a nest and a bird or two… ☺

This is where I get my name for making "wild & woodsy" wreaths!

This is the end of preparing your wreath with honeysuckle vines and mosses. But I think this preparation is a very important step that sets Ladybug wreaths and designs apart from others that you might see for sale in retail establishments.

Sure, this part does take some extra time, but it is well worth it. To start with a beautiful foundation like this, you can do anything you desire with your wreath!

Have you already purchased your greenery and stems of blooms you want to use in your wreath? This section with the honeysuckle has been fun and you probably want to run right out and purchase the supplies you need to continue. I hope so!

If you haven't purchased yet, then you can continue on until you reach the end of this part. Perhaps working through this first section has given you ideas about what stems, greenery and critters you want to add.

It is also my hope that, in starting with the honeysuckle and moss, you are not intimidated in the least at making your own wreath. I promise you, it really is not hard. Just take it step by step, don't rush yourself and you'll have a work of art when you are finished

If you think this part was fun, just wait! We're starting to add the colorful stems: Sunflowers, fruit, greenery, etc. You'll start seeing such a variety in your wreath now!

It will really begin to take shape and you'll want to run and hang it in your perfect spot before you finish, but wait, don't do it! Let's continue until it is completely finished! It will be BEAUTIFUL!!

Looking at this picture, I want you to notice the placement of the wreath and how the honeysuckle ends are looped throughout.

Since your grapevine wreath may be tight, put a pick on the end of the honeysuckle vine to create a sharp and fine point. Before any of the honeysuckle is cut, insert that end into your wreath and out the back about ½ inches to an inch.

At this point you can cut off the excess from the back. Secure it to a branch using a pipe cleaner (only use the pipe cleaner if the end doesn't fit in tightly), and then apply hot glue to the stem on the front and back just to make sure it doesn't slip out.

Look closely at my wreath. But I must warn you, no matter how hard you try, yours will not look exactly like this one. I wouldn't even be able to copy it myself. Unique and different is always BEST!

I just want you to understand the concept of letting the vine do what it does naturally! Then make sure each and every stem is secure and tight. Give it a gentle tug after the hot glue has dried to make sure.

If it is loose at all, apply more glue. Glue can be added until you get drips running out of the bottom of the wreath. That's okay; just make sure your hand it not in the way! Pick off the glue drips after they cool and dry. I would rather have to go back and pick drips off the bottom of your wreath, than have stems that might be loose and fall out!

In order to prevent glue drips, have a small pinch of moss to stick in on top of the hot glue before it runs out and down your wreath. Remember, by putting a little moss on each pipe cleaner, pick or stem that shows from the front, you will make the wreath look fuller and hide your work such as picks, glue, etc.

Moss is often the small touch that ties an entire wreath together. It may seem insignificant right now, but as your wreath unfolds, adding moss will fill gaps, add texture and make your wreath look more natural.

Here is a look at my workspace. I have all of my supplies right at my fingertips, making it convenient for me to work.   Notice the box of moss I have sitting to the left of the easel. It's already pulled apart into little pieces so that I can easily grab what I need (with one hand) without having to stop what I am doing.

Notice the easel in this picture? They are especially designed for Ladybug Wreaths and available for my customers to purchase. You'll LOVE the fact that it is fully adjustable, tilts forwards or backwards, as it allows your wreath to move up or down. I love working with my easel. http://ladybugwreaths.com/doorwreaths/easels

If you think you may be making more than one wreath, this easel will be an invaluable tool to help you! And believe me, if you have ever made a wreath lying flat on a table where you have to pick it up to see how it looks between inserting stems, this is invaluable. I would never make another wreath without one!

CHAPTER 4 – COMPLETE WITH SPONGE MUSHROOMS

Preserved mushrooms are an extra special way to make your wreaths look "wild & woodsy". These mushrooms are called "sponge" mushrooms and have been preserved and dyed green. I also love using the natural colored ones too!

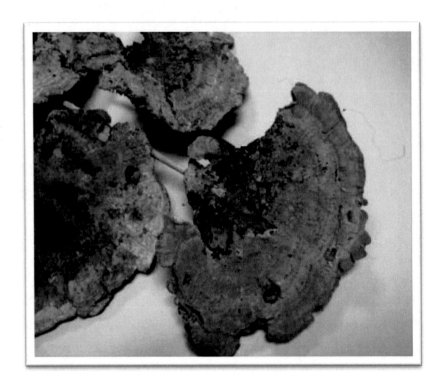

I love using them in my wreaths because they look so natural. These mushrooms are rough in texture and uneven because they grow wild on trees.

To order sponge mushrooms, Ladybug Wreaths sells our favorite supplies: www.LadybugWreathsCertified.com. They are well worth purchasing and, when inserted into your wreath creations, help you to reach that "wild and woodsy" look & feel.

Have you ever noticed flat mushrooms growing on an old tree? They are usually around the bottom, and they seem to kind of stagger, and stack on top of each other. When I use more than one in a wreath, I love creating that same effect. Then you have a nice little spot to hold a nest, a bird, or a clay pot.

After you add the honeysuckle's loops and curls, you have a little "hidden" spot that any bird would love to nest and hatch her eggs in. That's what this wild and woodsy look is all about - duplicating nature as much as possible.

So, I suggest that when a beautiful day comes along, take a walk in the woods near you, look at sticks, nests, mushrooms, and lichen – another form of moss. As you are looking at all of these wonders of nature, be thinking about how you can create a similar look in your designs, whether they are wreaths or arrangements.

You'll find that while you are out looking, you will discover some special things that would look absolutely adorable added to your wreath! Experiment a little and see what you can come up with. Then, let me know about your discoveries. I am so interested in seeing what new treasures you find in nature that will inspire you!

So, let's get busy adding these wonderful mushrooms! Most of the time, you're not able to pick the exact spot where your mushroom will seem to "settle in". It takes a little trial and error to finally find the spot where it really looks like it might be growing naturally there.

Also, if you already have lots of honeysuckle looped around, as I have in the above picture, it becomes a little more difficult, but well worth the time. For this reason, I almost never add glue to my mushroom stems before inserting them.

I just work with them a little while; pushing in the stems and pulling them back out. If it doesn't fit, then I might take it out and try it from the other side. It will eventually settle into the perfect spot, so just be patient and don't try to force it into a spot where it doesn't look like it belongs.

As soon as one fits into place, apply glue from the front and also on the stem sticking out the back, and then, of course, put that pinch of moss in from the front and back.

 As you remember, this helps secure your stem a little tighter, and also covers up the glue drips and the ugly mushroom stem which you don't want to show.

You probably need glue on the inside edge of the mushroom too, and any other place where it rests on the wreath.

In this close-up picture below, look at how much moss I added to the top-center of the mushroom, and also underneath.

Now, the second mushroom is being inserted lower, and at such an angle that the mushroom itself leans downward and is pointing up. Luckily this one slides right into place, as if it grew right there. Use the same gluing and mossing process here also.

When you turn your wreath around to add glue, cut off the mushroom stems, they will keep your wreath from hanging straight while working.

We only have one more mushroom to place. Where do you think it should go? At this point of design, it is a matter of preference, and also a matter of where it will fit in securely and look very natural.

CHAPTER 5 – SUNFLOWERS ARE A MUST

All right, let's start adding flowers. As a rule, I usually start with the largest flowers first. Now, that's not always the case. I just make that decision as I start each wreath.

In this extra-large wreath, I also have three very large Sunflowers, so I feel like it would be better to get those placed before adding other smaller flowers. The fillers and berries are always added last.

The Sunflowers and vivid bright yellow Gerber daisies make this wreath really pop with color. Aren't they pretty? Let's begin this step with the first Sunflower.

These three flowers have very long stems. Instead of cutting them, let's try curling them first.

Notice in the picture below, I am holding the Sunflower close to the wreath to see how it will fit. Because the stem is so long and thick, I decided to bend the Sunflower into a loose curl. I really would like to use the curled stem and not have to cut it.

Sunflower stems add to the "wild & woodsy" feel of this wreath, don't you think?

In this picture, I am bending the Sunflower into a tighter loop before I try to place it into the wreath again.

Twist and curl tightly because these stems really are thick and tough! Placing these stems can be tricky. Because they are so large, you want the Sunflowers to stick out from the wreath anywhere from ten to twelve inches.

I tried placing the first Sunflower stem into several different places on the wreath.

Here, I am tucking the long stem behind the honeysuckle loops I created along the bottom of my wreath. Do you like it there? I think I will try placing it in another spot before making my final decision.

Now, let's see how the Sunflower will look on the left side of the wreath.

Again, notice the way I have bent the stem to create a downward spiral curl. It is very important when you are designing your wreath to think through the placement of each stem before securing it with glue or pipe cleaners.

If you don't want your Sunflowers to stick out as far as mine, bend the stem more to add extra loops. Sometimes you might have to cut the stem off, if you can't find the perfect place for it to fit.

Even though my original plan was to leave my stem uncut, I finally had to use my wire cutters to cut off the end of the stem. After several attempts, I simply could not find the perfect spot for my flower without cutting it. Everyone has to change their plans – don't feel badly!

You can decide if you need to do likewise after placing the stem in different spots around the wreath.

I <u>finally</u> found the perfect location, and the Sunflower stem slid right in!

Sometimes, it takes a little work, but trying different places is always worth it! Because the stem is so large, I tied the Sunflower with a pipe cleaner in two places and secured it with glue.

It is important for you to tie all of the Sunflower stems and glue them in so they won't be loose or fall out. Remember to trim off any excess pipe cleaner stems as you go, so they won't be noticed.

Don't feel badly if you have to position a stem and take it back out several times.

If you have watched my videos before, you know that I sometimes take a stem back out several times before finding the perfect place for it.

A good quality pair of wire cutters is so very important. I buy mine at a home improvement center in the electrical department. They are eight inches long with a slight curve in the top. They are also kind of expensive, but work great, so are well worth it.

When a stem is as thick as the Sunflowers stems are, it is best to snip the wires individually instead of trying to cut them all at once. I don't have the strength to do that and perhaps you don't either!

Now it is time to place the second Sunflower stem. After you find the perfect spot, curl the stem or cut it to make it fit.

Here's another picture of me snipping at the big stem of this large sunflower. Sometimes they can really be stubborn, but just keep at it and you'll get it cut off.

Notice in the picture below, I am lifting up the bottom of the wreath to slide the stem to the side of the mushrooms, opposite from the other Sunflower stem. After the second stem is in place, again, secure it with a pipe cleaner and then apply hot glue.

Before we add our third Sunflower, I want to make sure the leaves of the first two look full and natural. If you had to cut off any excess length from your Sunflower stems as I did, this is a great time to add back any leaves that were cut off in the process.

Pick up the individual leaves, put a pick on each one, and wrap them in floral tape. Use hot glue to attach the individual leaves in the wreath, so they look natural on each Sunflower stem.

Have your container of moss nearby and add some moss where the pipe cleaners are showing through. I like to add moss throughout the entire wreath-making process behind flowers and to any open spots.

CHAPTER 6 – BIRD'S NEST, OH SO SWEET

Since we've been spending so much time at the lower part of the wreath, adding the mushrooms, Sunflowers, and moss, let's continue to focus our attention there.

In the picture below, I am holding a bird's nest and pick. If you would like for your nest to have feathers, simply look in your backyard for any that might have been left behind by birds.

Push the pick through the center of the woven nest at an angle, as I have done is this picture. Once the pick is halfway in, turn it over and apply hot glue around the bottom of the nest and down the end of the pick.

Place the nest into a naturally formed crook at the bottom section of the wreath. It would help to try it out without glue at first just to see if you can find the right spot.

When pushing the pick through the nest and into the wreath, sometimes you may run into one of the large wreath stems. Just rotate and slide it around a little to see if you can get it to slide in. It usually does pretty easily after a little experimenting.

If your nest is large, add another pick at the opposite angle and push it through the nest and into the wreath.

Both picks going at different angles really add strength so it will stay in place. Apply hot glue and a little moss around the nest so that it is secure on all sides.

Once the nest is in place, use your wire cutters to clip off the top and bottom of the pick (or picks).

If for some reason, the nest still doesn't feel secure, add more hot glue as needed. Feel free to add a little moss in the nest and trailing out the front side. Make it look like the Mama bird built the nest herself!

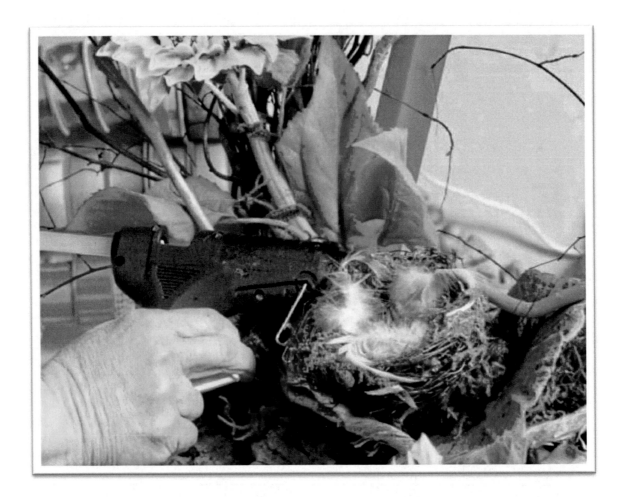

You can see in the picture above that my pipe cleaners are still showing on my Sunflower. This would be a great time to cover them up with moss.

 Just get a long narrow piece of moss, cover it with a little glue, and wrap it around the stem where the pipe cleaners are located. Make sure you add some behind also because that can show from the side.

Just thought this was such a sweet picture with the bird on her nest beside the Sunflowers!

CHAPTER 7 – NOT THROUGH WITH SUNFLOWERS

In the following pictures, look at how pretty the nest looks in my wreath! Any bird would be happy to make a home here!

Also notice how the honeysuckle naturally formed a crook for the nest to "nestle" into. This spot was not planned, and as a matter of fact, these kinds of things are close to impossible to plan, but it worked out perfectly, don't you think?

There always seems to be that perfect spot somewhere, you just have to look for it and be open to wherever it may be. It could be up near the top in the other loop.

Just study carefully the way your honeysuckle moves through your wreath. Don't force the nest into a spot where it looks unnatural, but be creative and keep looking until you find the "right" place.

I suppose you have noticed by now that I skipped over the third Sunflower and added my bird nest. While working with the second Sunflower, I spied the PERFECT spot for my bird nest, so I just could not resist it and had to stop and put it in. Now, to find the perfect place for our last Sunflower...

I cut my third Sunflower very short because it is going to be placed at the top of my wreath. Again, I used my wire cutters to snip the individual wires instead of trying to cut it all at once. These Sunflowers really do look lovely, but boy, they have really thick, tough stems!

Sunflowers always have a way of making me think of my childhood summer days. Their majestic beauty makes me smile. I remember them blowing in the breezes at my aunt and uncle's home. What do they make you think of?

This third and final Sunflower is going to proudly adorn the top of my wreath. Slightly off center, this stem balances the loop of honeysuckle I made on the opposite side.

Place your stem at the top of the wreath but not right in the middle. Notice it's face is leaning toward the right side and looking down a little upon my wreath.

Also notice in the picture above how each Sunflower stands out against the wreath. The one on the bottom protrudes out further than the others, which will add to the fullness of the wreath once it is finished.

I love it when things start to come together and I catch a glimpse of the final product! It is going to be absolutely beautiful!

Have you noticed those large green leaves that came on my Sunflower stems? Don't ever throw away unused leaves.

If you don't have room for them in this particular wreath, I know you'll need them in another wreath one day. I have a box that is dedicated solely to leaves. They make such a difference in your wreaths and I promise they will come in handy – if not now, then later!

Once your Sunflowers are in place, turn your wreath over and look for any stems that are poking out of the back. Even though I had cut my third stem short, it was still too long. And I also found a stick from my wreath that was sticking out a little too far. All of these will keep your wreath from hanging flat against the wall.

If you need to, take your wreath off of your easel like I did. Cut these stems off which are sticking out the back. It really helps to do this as you go along rather than waiting until the end and trying to get all of them off.

I had to pull out my heavy-duty wire cutters for this job. They have very long handles which give you more leverage when cutting these large heavy stems.

I really don't know what I would do without these. I don't use them often, but when I do, it is out of necessity. But it does take two people to use them. One person had to hold the wreath, and another is needed to hold onto both of the handles to do the cutting.

CHAPTER 8 – FRUIT PICKS FROM GARLANDS

I began this step by removing my fruit picks from a long fruit garland. This particular garland has five clusters of fruit, so it will be cut into 5 sections.

Your garland may have more or less clusters, but I would prefer for you to purchase picks, garlands, or fruit sprays rather than single pieces of fruit. The fruit and berries on garlands or sprays come on longer stems which give you the opportunity for the fruit stems to drape out and down away from the wreath.

I cut the garland into five sections and used three of them in my wreath. (I'm really upset because this particular garland has been discontinued, and I only have three left!) Isn't it so beautiful?

Below is a picture of the clusters that have been cut from the large garland.

A perfect location for the first fruit pick is the left side of the mushrooms and bird nest. I know that the color and texture of the fruit will look very pretty between the nest and the first Sunflower. It is a little hard to insert the stem into just the right location so I have to work at it a little, but persistence pays off and it goes into the exact spot.

I think you would really be surprised at how mixing so many colors together really makes your wreath show up. You know, I am talking about colors like pink and orange for example. Would you put them together in a wreath? Most people would not.

I would – with the right shades, of course.

Look at the color of the pomegranate. Doesn't it look so pretty up against the Sunflower? The cluster berries attached to this stem flow just perfectly out of the left bottom-side of this wreath. And the fig that is at the lowest point is so very sweet. Now I know it sounds kind of corny to call a fig sweet, but…. it really is!!

We are ready to choose the next spot for another cluster of fruit. I think the wonderful colors in these fruit picks need to be between each Sunflower in this particular wreath. This pattern will make the wonderful mix of colors flow all around.

CHAPTER 9 – GOTTA LEARN FLUFFING

If you're new to floral design, you are probably thinking, "What in the world is fluffing? Isn't that something I do to my hair?" Those of you who have designed florals before know exactly what I am talking about.

Every flower stem, ivy, fruit stem, etc., comes boxed up so tightly, that the branches, leaves, and blooms are closed, pointed upward, and lie flat against the stem. Packing it this way protects each stem during shipping.

When you get ready to use your stems you certainly don't want them to look like they just came out of the box. Failure to "fluff" makes for a flat and unattractive wreath. In this picture below, I am fluffing this fruit pick.

Do you remember the beautiful picture of the fruit garland at the beginning of this chapter? What you didn't see was me fluffing it to make it look full and vibrant.

The garland did not come out of the box already looking like that. I bent out each stem and curled open each leaf. I turned the face of each leaf outward, and opened up the stem so that it looked full and beautiful. This is called "fluffing."

You do a lot more fluffing when the Christmas season comes (or if your hair is flat… ☺) because of all the greenery. I discuss that further in my "Deck The Halls" Christmas book.

In the previous pictures, you saw where I added the second fruit pick. It is such a heavy stem, that I glued it in and tied the top of it with a pipe cleaner.   Don't forget to cover the pipe cleaner with a pinch of moss just like I did.

Normally, I would continue by adding the third fruit pick up on the top left between those two Sunflowers. But I am going to wait. This is a large space and I might want to add something else there also.

Instead, let's add some greenery before we decide exactly where to add the last of the fruit stems.

I still have that small honeysuckle loop up on the top left, and I want to make sure that I don't cover it up or hide it. I would really love to see a sweet little bird perched up in that loop. It will look so natural and woodsy, but we'll see how things turn out.

CHAPTER 10 – USING A FLORAL PICK

Lay the pick beside your flower or greenery stem so that the pick overlaps about one inch below the stem. Twirl the stem in the fingers of your left hand while wrapping the wire down the stem and onto the wood of the pick to bind them together.

Note: It is very important when using a floral pick that you wrap the wire VERY tightly. If you don't complete this step properly, the pick won't support your stem as you are pushing it into your wreath.

A loose pick would prevent your stem from being anchored properly into your wreath or arrangement.

Picks come in several sizes. I always try to keep three sizes on hand at all times. A two and one-half inch pick, which is the size you see in the above pictures, is my favorite and the size most used in wreaths. A four-inch pick is good if you need just a little more length when inserting a stem into your wreath, and where you need it to extend out from the wreath a little more.

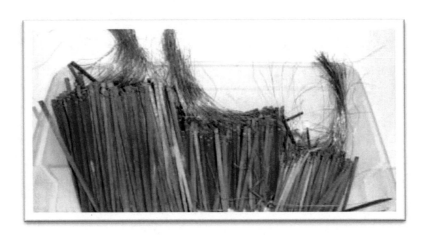

The six-inch pick is very good to have on hand. I don't really use it that often, but when I need it, nothing else will do. I always use the six-inch picks when anchoring a bird nest even if it sticks out the back when I am finished. I just cut off the excess and know that my nest will not come out. And then there are times when you have a very thick sturdy stem that needs a pick. I always use the six-inch for these mainly because it has more wire attached and I am going to need a longer piece of wire when wrapping it around both stems.

I thought you might like to see how I store my picks on my work counter. They are in a very inexpensive clear plastic container and I have them lined up by size. This makes it very easy for me to grab the size pick I need without spreading them all over my counter, adding to the mess I probably already have!

CHAPTER 11 – USING FLORAL TAPE

You must always wrap florist tape on your stem after applying a pick – it keeps your wire secure and also provides support to the joint.

Apply the florist tape by starting at the top of the pick, and in a curling motion, bring it down the stem. Wrap the tape around itself a couple of times at the beginning and at the end.

When using florist tape, keep a slight pull on it while wrapping. This stretch makes it stick to itself and stay in place.

Florist tape is not typically sticky. This tape only sticks to itself, you must stretch it a little to make it stick together easier.

Floral tape comes in several shades of brown and green that looks natural against your birch wreath.

There is no need to wrap floral tape on a stem that does not have a pick, unless the tip is frayed and can't be inserted it into your wreath.

CHAPTER 12 – GREENERY

Let's look at a picture of the entire wreath to see exactly how it looks up at this stage of its creation.

You might think that we are just about finished, but we still have a ways to go in order for the wreath to look "wild and woodsy". The greenery you are about to add will make such a difference to this already beautiful wreath!

Adding greenery is an important step. Let's start with fluffing - opening up and curling the wisteria stem. Bend it into the shape you would like to see it flowing out of the wreath.

I used three different types of greenery in this wreath. It is perfectly fine if you would like to use more than three kinds – I do all the time!

Different textures and styles work best – the more, the better. For example, in this wreath, I am using a stem of ficus leaves, trailing ivy, left-over leaves, eucalyptus stems along with different grasses.

a. FICUS

Let's begin by adding a long stem of ficus leaves. You can find these exact leaf stems I use in my Amazon supply store: http://ladybugcertified.com/store/ .

With this type of a long leaf stem, you can create a large and airy look for your wreath by placing these stems radiating out from your wreath. Using a mix of greenery gives your wreath depth and a lush appearance.

If you are using a stem that is similar to my ficus leaf stem, use your wire cutters to cut the stem into five sections, or less.

If you need some shorter stems, you can then cut some of these in half.

Apply a generous but not dripping stream of glue down the stem or the wrapped pick, and insert it into the very top of the wreath first.

It is very important to check each stem as you progress to make sure they are very secure before going on to another. This building process is like laying a very strong and sturdy foundation.

I placed the first stem in the very top of my wreath. You can see it in the picture above. If you take a look at some of the wreath examples I have on my web site, www.ladybugwreaths.com, you'll see that I always add some sort of greenery radiating out of the top and then the bottom just to give the wreath some height.

If you don't do this, your wreath will have somewhat of a flat appearance on the top. It just doesn't show up as well this way.

Greenery is not the only stem I add coming out of the top, as you will see in later chapters.

Here, I am adding more of ficus to the bottom of the wreath. I decided not to cut it up as much as I had first planned.

I want this wreath to look very large, full, and wild, so the longer ficus stems will certainly give me that look. You can also use your ivy trailing down this far or any other greenery that you may have purchased.

Even fern fronds will give you a little different, but similar look.
Speaking of fern fronds, those give you another very good alternative to
mixed greens in whatever floral you are working on.

Look at the difference in the bottom of this beautiful wreath after I
added the leafy greens. It really makes such a difference. Without the
greenery radiating out from the wreath like it does, you would have a
tight and stuffy appearance.

Again, as in putting in previous stems, I am running a generous stream of glue down each stem, and then immediately inserting the stem at an angle into my wreath.

As always, have your moss already pulled apart and ready to grab with one hand so you can stuff it in and catch any glue drips before they run all the way down. This process really does anchor your stem in tightly and covers up any drips of glue that are starting to run.

In this picture, greenery has been added to the top and bottom of the wreath. In fact, don't be afraid to add just as much greenery swooping out the sides of your wreath.

When you are adding your greenery, this is the time to decide what shape you would like for your wreath to be.

If I want a perfectly round wreath (no matter what shape my original wreath started out as), I would add wisteria and other greens coming out on the sides just as far, if not further, than they radiated out from the bottom and the top.

This is a critical part right here that I want you to understand. You really do not want all of your stems to come out from the wreath at the exact same distance all around. Some should be longer, and some should be shorter. Some should curl forward, and some should curl backward.

What I do want is for you to hang your wreath on a white door or wall, and step back away from it. Take a look at the overall effect and make sure that you are getting the approximate shape you would like for your wreath to end up with. This decision is hard to make when you are standing up very close to your wreath while working.

From time to time, my Ladybug designers and I stop several times during the wreath-making process to do what we call a **"door check"**. We remove our wreaths from the easels we work on, and hang them on a white door. We step back and any flaws immediately show up.

You should try it, you'll be surprised!!

CHAPTER 13 – GRASSES

Now, let's add the grasses. These long stems of grass come in a bunch and are cut off by the stem. Several types of grasses are available to you in my Amazon supply store: http://ladybugcertified.com/store/

I suggest that you purchase at least two different kinds of grasses. Some should be long, and some can be shorter. It's also okay if they have a little color added to them – sometimes that helps. The grass we are using in this extra-large example is the longer grass. Since it is so long, it will continue to add to the "wild and airy" look that we already started with the ficus leaves.

Notice how the different styles and textures of greenery add interest to the wreath. Move all around your wreath adding stems of grass, as you like.

Some of the grass will drape toward the inside of the wreath, while some hang towards the outside. You want them to be wild, loose, airy, and free looking. Don't place all of them on the exact same side of your wreath.

For variation, point some in toward the front and some in toward the back. Typically, I like to make the grass at the bottom swoop out even more to give my wreaths that "wild and woodsy" look that I love so very much.

I think it's time to take a look again at a larger picture and see where we have gotten to so far. In the following picture, look at how the grasses are swooping in different directions.

Notice the grass stem on the right side near the bottom. This one is draped in toward the center of the wreath.

Look how pretty!

Now, and again, later on during this wreath-making process, I will be adding extra grasses anywhere I see a need for an airier, wilder look.

If you haven't checked out the wreaths and other information products on my websites yet, I encourage you to do so.

http://ladybugwreaths.com/doorwreaths/

http://ladybugcertified.com/

Next, I'll be talking about an easel made exclusively for Ladybug Wreaths! I came up with the design, and then had a friend to hand make each one just for you… and me! ☺

The next picture below shows how the top of my easel is adjustable. When I need to work on the bottom of the wreath, I simply move the adjustable pin up to an upper hole which will raise the wreath up even higher.

This gives me full access to the bottom without bending and stooping. I also love the fully adjustable back that allows me to work at any angle I am most comfortable with.

Next, you'll see a picture of my favorite, one-of-a-kind, easel!

I designed this easel after too many disasters with an old easel that refused to stand up on its own. I almost broke my neck on it several times! LOL!!

These easels are custom made and come with very simple assembly. If you take one of my workshops, you receive one absolutely FREE!

CHAPTER 14 – GERBER DAISIES

Aren't these flame-colored Gerber daisies dazzlingly, bright and beautiful? The flame color matches reds, oranges, and pinks. I usually call this color "tearose", but its official name is "flame".

The daisy stems are long and can be curled very easily, thus making them radiate out from the wreath for a loose, airy feel.

In this picture, I am adding a couple of daisies in the upper left of the wreath. I will fill in this spot with fruit later. When you have a large space left in your creation, Gerbers look especially good if you can cluster them together. I really want to get my colors spread throughout evenly.

Notice in this picture how dramatic these two Gerber daisies are together.

I have inserted one at an angle with the face of the flower looking to the right. The second daisy is inserted a little to the left with the face of the flower looking up and left a little.

It looks best if the flower heads turn away from each other. This color really works well with the Sunflowers and the fruit we have already used. Doesn't it just do something for you!?! Sounds strange, Huh? Colors really are great!

Let's talk about picking out your flowers for a few minutes.
When you are picking out the flowers that you would like to use in your wreath, spend some time walking around the store and holding each stem you like in your hand.

You will be able to tell very quickly if you have the **"right"** combination – it will just **"grab"** you and you'll say, **"That's it"**! If you are uncertain about the combination, or if your mix doesn't really grab you, you need to work at it some more by putting some stems back and adding new ones.

After 20 plus years of designing wreaths, I still do that very thing in my shop. Sometimes I know right away which combinations will go together, but other times, I really have to work at it to get that "**wow appeal**".

While we're looking at this picture, I would like to point out how airy every stem in this wreath is so far.

Some of the pieces of fruit are a little closer to the wreath, but as a whole, all of the flowers and greenery are swooping in one direction or another away from the wreath.

This movement is classic in my wreaths, contributing to the reason my style is called "wild and woodsy". I'm sure you have seen wreaths that looked as if the flower heads were pulled off and glued directly into the wreath.

Well, you certainly won't find our wreaths looking like that! By using each stem in a wild and airy way, we are essentially bringing nature together in our wreath in a way that looks…well… natural!

Now, after saying what I just said on the previous page, there are some exceptions to that rule.

There will always be spots in your wreath where you are going to need some bold bright color up pretty close to the wreath. And this is why I am NOW PLACING THIS Gerber right in behind this cluster of fruit. Looks pretty there, doesn't it?

With each and every stem I am placing in my wreath, I am applying glue down the stem first, and then adding it, or I am placing the stem, and then applying glue with the tip of my glue gun. You will have to make this decision as you go.

The exact placement of your stem will depend on how loose or tight your space is. And typically, the bottom of your wreath fills up with glue and moss pretty quickly making it hard to insert your stems. Just keep trying and they'll go in! Sometimes using a sharp pick works better than a blunt flower stem.

As I am placing my Gerber daisy stem, I like to place a slight curl on the stem before cutting and placing it. With my thumb on the inside of the stem, and a couple of fingers on the outside, I run my fingers down the stem applying pressure from the inside.

This pressure makes your stem curl slightly. The stems in your wreath always look so much more natural and "real" if they are curled slightly in and out rather than being very straight.

In the picture below, I am cutting the Gerber after holding it up to the wreath to determine exactly how long the stem should be.

I think I will have this one curling out the left side of my wreath. There is some empty space there and I also would like for my wreath to look a little wider.

As we discussed before, you can actually control the exact size of your finished wreath by placement of stems, no matter what the size or shape of the grapevine or birch wreath you started with.

You don't even need to worry if your wreath looks a little squashed on one side or is not perfectly round or oval. A good floral designer, which I am confident you will become, can make the wreath come out looking like the exact shape she (or he) wants just by stem placement. Don't worry, I promise with practice you will arrive there!

In this picture, I am inserting the Gerber to the left side as we already discussed. There! This will really give me some of the width I need for my wreath. Of course, I wouldn't leave it hanging out there all by itself.

Other stems, such as the Verbena, grasses, and ficus leaves help to fill in spaces around it. As I finish anchoring this stem with some generous glue and tucking a pinch of moss in beside the stem very tightly, I am certain it will not be coming out.

Now, I'll turn the face a little more toward the front of the wreath. Just think of how you see so many flower "faces" in nature turning toward the sun. That is exactly how these Gerbers, as well as any other stem of flowers you should choose, need to look.

These are the "faces" that will greet your many admirers when you place this beautiful wreath on your front door or a special place in your home. Get ready for the compliments!

Just remember, we don't ever want any stems sticking straight out from your wreath, like the spokes from the center of a wagon wheel. The slightest curl and bend in your flower stem can give your creation that soft, natural look and make such a difference!

When I say I am tucking a pinch of moss in beside the stem very tightly, it is often because there is a lot of extra space where I want to insert my stem. I use a piece of moss large enough to hold this stem against the wreath, effectively closing up the extra space.

After adding glue to one side of that piece of moss, I carefully push it in with my finger, and hold it tightly until I am sure it has dried. **Please be careful doing this!** Keep your fingers away from direct contact with the hot glue. I've had many burns that way!

This is a very sweet close-up picture of the bottom, center of my wreath. It always helps to make sure this area is full of details. For example, the bird nest is in the center, and on the left side I have the multi-colored fruit pick tucked up very closely.

On the right side, you'll find other fruit. Still, I don't think that is enough color. So I have decided to add another Gerber daisy very close to the right side of the nest, pointing forward. Now, the bottom of our wreath is aglow with bright, bold, beautiful colors!

I also like for this to be a very woodsy area of our wreath...with honeysuckle vine, mushrooms, and the nest. At the same time, though, this area can be very detailed with lots and lots of color.

In this close-up view, you can see the sweet pink raspberries dangling down and the green/rose cluster berries adding so much to this scene!

Then, when our sweet, colorful bird is added...well...it is just PERFECTION!

The last Gerber to be added is measured and cut as we have done before. I like to leave some length on it so that the flower will stand out from the wreath. Can you tell where this one is needed? I think it needs to be curling out of the bottom of this beauty!

How about hanging down low between the Sunflower and the fig? There are already greens there but some additional color is definitely needed. We'll cut the stem so that it will hang out much lower than even the Sunflower and curl up toward the front. Insert it just as we have done with the other stems before, using glue and moss.

Here is where you might need to turn your wreath upside down and away from you so that you can get it inserted and glued securely before hanging your wreath back up. And don't worry about turning your wreath upside down. You have built this one securely from the ground up, so nothing will fall out!

CHAPTER 15 – VERBENA AND/OR BERRIES

Now let's add the Verbena stems. There are typically four blooms in each of my stems, but whatever medium size flower you buy might have more or less blooms on each.

I really like for this size flower to radiate out from the wreath as much as possible, so think about that when purchasing your smaller, accent flowers and make sure they have somewhat longer stems. Cut these into individual blooms to be spread throughout your wreath.

If you cannot find Verbena or a medium size accent flower, you can get the same effect with a pretty berry stem. So, you might want to keep that in mind when shopping.

In this picture, you can see where I have inserted my Verbena stems. The Verbena I used is about the same color as the Gerber daisies, but they are smaller, and their texture is more airy.

Since the flowers are the same color as the Gerbers, place your Verbena or berry stems in places that need more color.

As you can see in the previous picture, I placed a stem on the left side of the wreath so that it bends over the bird's nest. I then moved around the wreath, placing stems so that they stood out from the wreath providing a pop of color in empty spots.

Remember to secure your stems with glue and, if needed, add moss. Doesn't the wreath look perfectly lovely? The use of large and small flowers provides so much contrast and interest to the wreath.

These tiny purple berry clusters in the picture above are just delightful in any wreath! They add so much color and texture! Stick them up close and around your nest, mushrooms, or stems.

You will need to use your wire cutters to separate the berries into individual stems. They are really so very pretty wherever I tuck them.

As you can see below, I am adding the first one right beside and behind the bird nest. It will look like this sweet bird built her nest among these berries!

When shopping for your stems, look for some sort of cluster berries like these. If you cannot find them, you can get the same effect with a cluster of smaller flowers that you can tuck in and around your focal points, and anywhere else in your wreath that needs extra color and texture.

Here, I have placed a small cluster of purple berries directly behind the bird's nest. This splash of color, along with the Verbena and the pomegranate, will direct your eyes to the nest and all of the details we have put in that area.

This illustrates exactly what I was explaining on the page before. Notice how the round pomegranate, purple Verbena, and the draping, pretty red raspberries all draw attention to the bird's nest. The different colors, shapes, and textures really add something, don't you think?

I want to take a moment here to show you a side view of this wreath so far. If you look closely at the picture, you can tell that some of the side stems are tucked in a little toward the front of the wreath, while others are tucked in toward the back.

Also, they curl at different angles, from the front, the back and the side.

In this picture, I tucked some purple berry clusters tightly into the top of the wreath. I also decided to add some more ficus leaves to create extra fullness in this area.

Some people like to see a lot of the birch wreath showing and some do not. This is a personal preference. You can decide just how much of the wreath you want to reveal, and then let that lead you as to how many items you place up close to your wreath.

If you have any wisteria or other greens left, feel free to add some wherever you see the need.

I curled the wisteria toward the center of the wreath so it wasn't left standing straight up in the air. Instead of adding the rest of my purple berries at this point, I think I will set them aside and add the stems throughout the process as I see fit.

CHAPTER 16 – BIRDS OF A FEATHER

Begin by cutting off the wires of the feet of the bird and, as a matter of fact, you could cut the feet off also (yes, I said the feet!) with your wire cutters. As cute as the feet are, they just don't show when you put her into the nest.   She actually sits in place better without them.

The bird is made out of a soft foam material. This makes it easy to insert the pointed end of a small pick into the bottom of the bird. Cut off the bottom half of the pick (the end with the wire) at an angle so that it will go into the wreath easier.

Apply some glue to the stem of the pick and the bottom of the bird. Push it through the woven nest. Be careful, this much glue will really get you! If it should, just run cold water over your hand until the glue peels off carefully. Don't try to peel it off yourself, just let the cold water do it.

The nests are sometimes tightly woven, so you may have to move your bird around a little to find the right spot. Press the bird tightly into the nest and hold it until the glue has dried.

Another way of doing this is to push a pick into your nest, picking out an easy spot to insert it, before you reach over with a bird that is already dripping with glue. I suggest that you hold your bird down with pressure until the glue has dried.

On delicate spots like this, where the item you are working with could be knocked off easily, you need to pay a little more attention and perhaps take a bit more time. Maybe even shoot some more glue in with your glue gun and apply moss in areas that don't show from the front of the bird.

Now that your bird is secured into its nest, let's add the leftover purple berries under the front side of the nest. Another great place to add some berries is out the top left side of the nest. Notice in the picture below how all of the berries add a pop of color around the bird.

That is such a beautiful sight! Look closely at this picture and examine how the center, bottom of the wreath really draws your eye to everything that is going on there like the mushrooms, the nest, the bird, and a great assortment of berries, fruit, and mixed colors.

Now that your first bird is securely placed, let's find a special home for your other bird. I think the top loop of honeysuckle will be the perfect spot, don't you? Because the honeysuckle sticks out from the wreath, I want to make sure the vine has a secure place to hold my bird.

I create a safe spot by gluing moss to the top and bottom of one side of the honeysuckle vine. Make sure you press the moss together tightly from the top and the bottom sort of creating a tiny mossy mound or little shelf for the bird, and hold it securely until the glue has dried.

After cutting off the wires and feet of the second bird, apply hot glue to its bottom and press it tightly onto the moss glued to the honeysuckle vine. Do not place a pick in this bird! We are relying on the hot glue to hold the bird on the vine instead of a pick. In the above picture, you can see where I am holding it tightly onto the spot until the glue has dried and you are certain the bird is secure. I think my red bird looks happy sitting there. How does yours look?

Now that our second bird is securely placed on the honeysuckle vine, let's add some more purple berries to our wreath.

In this picture, I just tucked a bunch of berries behind the top right Sunflower. It is a small tight spot, but the burst of color adds lots of interest.

Continue around your wreath, adding the rest of your purple berries and Verbena stems. At this point, it is a good idea to look under and around the fruit, stems, and berries. We don't want to overlook a spot that may show up from the side, even though you can't see it from the front. Also, look underneath just in case it hangs high over a mantle.

Here is a picture of our wreath at the end of this step. Doesn't it look just lovely! Can you believe that we still have more stems to add in order to complete this "wild and woodsy" wreath? And, yes, there is plenty of room for them, even though it doesn't look like it.

I hope at this point, you are feeling very comfortable deciding where certain stems should be placed. Your own creativity will begin to show more and more as I continue to guide you as we add more fillers, and yes… our special critters!

Start taking some liberties of your own. If you see a spot where you might like a certain color or stem, please go ahead, and try your wings.

We have been through a long lesson, and I personally think you could finish it by yourself now, but I won't ask you to do that just yet.

I'm sure you're beginning to see just how much of a building process this is. By taking your time and adding one stem or bloom at a time, you are designing a very special wreath that will last for years.

Oh, and by the way, I have probably used 3 or 4 long glue sticks by now; so don't be afraid to use what you need.

CHAPTER 17 – MORE GREENS AND FRUIT

As I stepped back to carefully examine my wreath, I noticed a spot on the top of the wreath, toward the back, that needed more greenery. In this picture, I am adding another ficus stem to fill in.

Now, let's add another fruit pick. This time, I am going to cut up the pick into individual pieces of fruit so they can be dispersed throughout the wreath where color is needed. I placed an apple, using a pick and glue gun, to the left side of the wreath above a Sunflower. You can do the same.

Now let's add some more grass to our wreath. (We will get back to the fruit in just a bit, I promise!) By placing a stem of grass toward the front of the wreath so that it drapes forward, we have added fullness to this particular spot.

Back to the fruit we just cut into pieces. I want to tuck a yummy looking pear into the top of the wreath, but first I need a pick.

Don't forget the important step of adding a pick to your stems and then wrapping them with floral tape. We want to be assured that each piece of fruit or stem has been securely placed in your wreath.

If your fruit does not come with a stem, all you have to do is stick the sharp end of a long pick into your fruit and add glue where it enters. Let this dry a minute and then cut the other stem of the pick off into a point. It is then ready to insert in your wreath.

Want to add some airy yellow filler? This lovely yellow filler looks wonderful on the top of my wreath next to the purple berries, a Verbena stem, and beside the Sunflower.

Fillers do exactly what they are called. They "fill" any empty spots you might have in your wreath. They also add a nice contrasting color, don't you think?

All along the right side of your wreath, add your filler stems where you think they will look best. Make sure they stand out and add to the "wild" look.

These airy filler stems make the wreath appear larger and fuller without making it look stuffy. Reserve some filler for the other side of your wreath.

I think we need to place some filler on the top of the wreath. Allow it to radiate out, creating that larger appearance we just talked about. Continue to add the filler stems to the left side of the wreath and the top, working your way down to the bottom and the center of your beauty!

Fillers don't dominate any part of the wreath; they complement the other flowers and colors in the wreath.

I want to add some of this pretty yellow color coming right out from under the bird nest. I am sure by now; you have gotten the hang of it.

Just go around your wreath looking for empty and colorless spaces and add pieces of your stems that you may have left over. You don't have to put too much. If you don't see any spots, then hold what you have left over for your next wreath!

CHAPTER 18 – FINISHING TOUCHES

We have almost completed creating our large and beautiful wreath! You should be really proud of your wreath… I know I am.

Now, let's start adding our finishing touches! These details may seem rather unimportant, but truthfully, it's the little touches that give my wreaths that extra special quality.

Any critters you place, whether it's a ladybug, bumblebee, grasshopper, or even a dragonfly, will add whimsy, character and delight to your work. Gather together your little critters. As you can see in the picture of the bee, I start by gently pulling the legs of my bumblebee apart.

Unlike the birds we added earlier, the legs of the bumblebee are important for securing the bug to the wreath. Large bugs take a little more glue so make sure that they are properly secured. I decided to place this critter on a piece of honeysuckle vine located on the left side of my wreath. You can add him wherever you would like.

Just make sure the bee is placed in a spot where he can be seen. There's no point adding a bee if you can't find him! My clients love finding them sitting on the honeysuckle vine or tucked beside a prominent flower.

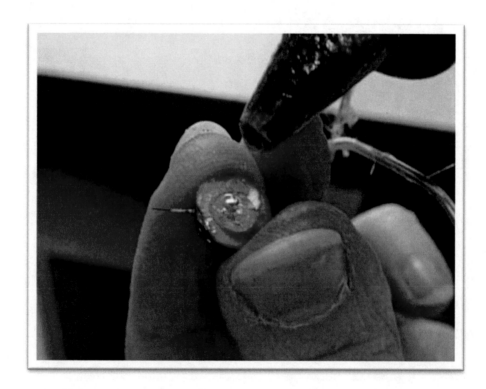

I really like the idea of placing my ladybug near the bird's nest.

As you can see in the following picture, I think the ladybug deserves a little recognition, so I made sure to put her in a prominent place in my wreath. The honeysuckle vine near the nest will be just perfect! Add a drop of glue to the back of the critter and place her on the vine.

Make sure it is secure before moving on to the next step. At this point, you can add any other critters you purchased.

HERE ARE CLOSEUP VIEWS OF OUR LADYBUG AND BUMBLEBEE!
(Do you see them?)

Hmmm…. the wreath looks like it could be complete at this point. Let's take a moment to carefully look over it and see if there is anything we need to take care of.

An empty spot might need some moss? Or even a touch of color from a filler stem? How are your greens looking? We don't want to leave any section that is not completely finished. After some careful thought, I've decided to add a couple more finishing touches.

We always joke at this point, "We could really leave it and walk away and have an absolutely beautiful wreath!" There seems to always be "just one more" stem to add, or "just one more" thing to be done.

You just have to pick the moment when you say, ***"That's it!!! It is absolutely beautiful, and I am finished!"***

I need to add some more greenery to make this wreath look just perfect! We are after that "wild and woodsy" look, so don't hold back from making your wreath look fuller and wilder. I'm adding a stem of Eucalyptus leaves in the picture below.

Use any greenery you may have left over. If you have any sprigs or little blooms left from your collection of supplies, this is a great time to add them.

Glue these blooms where you see a place that needs a little color. Just be creative as to where you put yours! But, like I said before, it is always hard to find a stopping point. Don't get carried away here and add too much. That's easy to do!

Let's also add some extra moss. I tucked some moss under a few stems on the top left side of the wreath that looked a little bare. Tuck any left-over moss in and around your wreath where you see stems or picks peeking out.

Next is a picture of the completed wreath! I think it looks wonderful!

All of the colors and textures mix together so well! It is even better, fuller, and wilder than I had hoped! The subtle finishing touches we've added will change your wreath from a "homemade" feel into the polished, professional appearance that you want.

Before this wreath is ready to hang on your front door, we must cut off all the stems which are poking out from the back of the wreath.

You really don't want anything rough poking through your wreath which may scratch a door or even a storm door.

CHAPTER 19 – CLEANING UP THE BACK

Turn your wreath over to the back. Use your wire cutters to remove any stems or picks that are sticking out of your wreath.

Sometimes you have to use a little force, so don't be afraid to get in there and work it! It is very important for your wreath to lie flat against your door when you hang it.

Removing any stems or picks that poke out of the back will help you accomplish that. It is also one of the finishing steps to ensure your wreath will have that professional, rather than homemade, look to it.

While I was trimming the back of the wreath and could get a good look at the back of it, I realized that the back, bottom section needed to be covered with some moss. I turned my wreath upside down and finished the underside.

If you hang a wreath up over a mantle or fireplace, you can see up and under your wreath, so make sure you finish the underneath also, if it will be hanging where anyone can see it.

It's time to do a "door check"! It looks great to me, how about you?

Countless times, I have been pleased with my work when it was on an easel, but after seeing it hang on a door, I wasn't. Sometimes the shape isn't round or the greenery is lopsided. I know this may sound funny to you, because I'm the lady who LOVES the "wild & woodsy" wreaths. But I can also be really funny about a wreath that looks lopsided! ☺

When this happens, I put the wreath back on the easel and add whatever is necessary to get that polished look.

So, before you put all of your supplies away, make sure you do a door check! It can really make a difference! And if you notice a problem, go back and add moss or greenery so that your wreath looks absolutely perfect!

CONGRATULATIONS!!!!!!

Congratulations!!!

You have just completed a beautiful wreath!!

The unique design and vibrant colors will attract compliments from everyone who comes to your door.

I have enjoyed getting to know you and visit with you as we have worked "side by side" on this special project! If you are a returning customer, I hope the design process has gotten easier for you.

I am certainly looking forward to us working together again very soon!

Smiles & Blessings...Nancy

APPENDIX - RESOURCES

LADYBUG NEWSLETTER

Nancy's **FREE** weekly newsletter contains: decorating ideas; design tips; free 'how to' videos; or special deals. To begin receiving Nancy's newsletter, go to her website: http://www.LadybugWreaths.com .
Nancy would LOVE to add you to her mailing list!

INSTRUCTIONAL DVDS & DIGITAL VIDEOS

Nancy offers MANY instructional videos that show you step by step how to make a particular style of wreath or bow. To view the list of video offerings, go to:

http://ladybugwreaths.com/doorwreaths/product/dvds/
http://ladybugwreaths.com/doorwreaths/download-videos/

WORKSHOPS:

Nancy offers both private and group workshops in her studio in South Carolina. In these workshops you receive personal instruction from Nancy and her assistant on the art of wreath making. You leave with the most beautiful wreath you created and with the knowledge how to make more!

Learn more here:
http://passionintoprofits.com/workshops/

COACHING:

Nancy, along with her friend and partner, Linda Joseph, offer private and group coaching. Our goal is to show you step by step how to sell your wreaths and/or other creations online.

Getting Started Coaching

Many ladies want help turning their creations into a business. "Best of Nancy" is our introductory coaching club. It consists of a forum, video training, monthly updates and bonuses. The forum is a great place to ask questions, meet other like-minded people and find encouragement. The video training covers all the essential elements for selling your creations on the Internet.
To learn more go to:
www.BestofNancy.com

We also offer extended workshops:
www.PassionIntoProfits.com/workshop2/

Purchase My Favorite Supplies From Ladybug Wreaths

Another Ladybug Wreath's site, **www.LadybugCertified.com** provides the exact same supplies Nancy uses in all her wreaths. Available from Amazon, shipping is FREE with Amazon Prime. Benefits are…no Sales Tax ID is required; no case quantities; no minimums; and super-fast shipping.

PURCHASE CUSTOM WREATHS

Nancy continues to create beautiful wreaths that are a treasure for any home. To see her wreaths currently for sale go here:
http://ladybugwreaths.com/doorwreaths/wreaths-for-sale-2/

To order a custom wreath, go here:
http://ladybugwreaths.com/doorwreaths/custom-door-wreaths/

CONNECT WITH NANCY ON FACEBOOK

https://www.facebook.com/nancyladybugwreaths

SUMMARY

How to Make a Gorgeous Wreath

- Reports- http://passionintoprofits.com/free-reports/
- Workshops - http://passionintoprofits.com/workshop1/
- Physical DVDs – http://LadybugCertified.com
- Digital Videos - http://ladybugwreaths.com/doorwreaths/download-videos/

Where to Find the Best Supplies

- Wreath Supplies – http://LadybugCertified.com
- Secret Vendor List – http://MySecretVendors.com

How to Sell Online

- Reports- http://passionintoprofits.com/free-reports/
- Passion Into Profits Coaching – http://PassionIntoProfits.com
  - Best of Nancy Membership – http://BestofNancy.com
  - Workshops - http://passionintoprofits.com/workshop2/

APPENDIX – GETTING STARTED MAKING WREATHS

THREE EASY STEPS TO MAKE YOUR FIRST GORGEOUS WREATH

1. **Get Step by Step Instructions**

2. **Buy Supplies**

3. **Make a Wreath**

STEP 1 - GET STEP BY STEP INSTRUCTIONS

I have produced well over 50 step by step instructional video tutorials and have written several instructional e-Books! The feedback I have received has been overwhelming! Here is just one testimonial:

> *"Nancy, I have just viewed my copy of your video about the two-foot Christmas tree, and I cannot tell you how much I treasured every moment of it!!! I received it a couple of days ago but put it aside until I had time to savor every minute of it like I was eating a luscious box of chocolates! I love your color choices, and not only did your tree have a wonderful burst of elegant color and glitter, but hanging the greens made the tree have movement as well. You REALLY are a Master Designer and I could watch your video all day.*
>
> *I shared your website with a professional wedding, floral designer. She was thrilled with your website and had as much of a hard time dragging herself away from it as I did!*
>
> *Thank you SO much for pursuing your heart's work through your adversities because it is a real inspiration to so many of us too!"*
> *Blessings! ~Carmela~*

[NOTE: I have hundreds of testimonials. If you'd like to read a few more, click here. http://ladybugwreaths.com/doorwreaths/how-to-make-wreaths-testimonials/]

You have just purchased the Sunflower Garden e-Book to learn how to make a wreath. How much easier do you think it would be to "watch" me while I do it and explain what I am doing? Yes, it would help a whole lot!

You have two ways to learn from me:

1. Watch one of my many instructional videos

2. Let me teach you in person in my studio!

INSTRUCTIONAL VIDEO

Rather than give you a list of my DVD's to choose from, I want to make this very easy!

To get started:
Just purchase 2 DVDs: "Summer Daze" and "Ribbons and Bows" [http://ladybugwreaths.com/doorwreaths/product/dvds/dvd-summer-daze/ and http://ladybugwreaths.com/doorwreaths/product/dvds/how-to-make-a-bow-for-wreaths/]

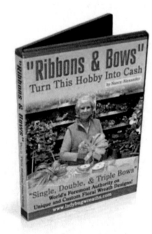

Summer Daze   **Ribbons & Bows**

All you have to do is watch these two videos! You'll be surprised at how much you learn!

LEARN FROM ME (NANCY) IN PERSON!

Have you ever just wanted to have Nancy stand by your side and show you step by step how to make a wreath?

Well, now you can attend a workshop in her studio!

- **Spend the day with Nancy**
- **Learn in person from Nancy**
- **Immediate feedback from Nancy**

That's right! You can come to my personal shop and learn directly from me! We will start the day at 9:00am in my shop. You will work on your own wreath as I and my assistant lead in the design of a gorgeous wreath.

I provide all the supplies and tools and even an easel. You will be able to ask me any question you want and I will give you immediate feedback on your work. You will complete a 24 inch wreath.

You will learn to ship by boxing and shipping your wreath to your home. You finish the workshop around 4pm with a completed wreath and all the tools, as well as the bonuses.

Learn more about my workshops!
[http://passionintoprofits.com/workshop1/]

STEP 2 – BUY SUPPLIES

You will need some basic supplies for making wreaths.

These wreath making materials include:

- "Wild Birch" wreaths in several sizes made exclusively for LadybugWreaths
- Wreath making easel designed by and made exclusively for LadybugWreaths
- Rolls of freshly harvested honeysuckle vine
- Klein Wire Cutters, my personal favorite
- Sure-bonder Glue Gun or any other hot glue gun

The above is a picture of some of the supplies you will need to get started. You will also need a wreath form (birch or grapevine), honeysuckle vine, and an easel (optional).

WREATH SUPPLIES

I am so excited to announce that due to an overwhelming demand, we have started to provide my favorite supplies for making wreaths.

These are not just any supplies you can buy at the local craft store. No Ma'am!
These are the supplies that I, Nancy Alexander, use in my high end wreaths!

Our store will grow, but here are just a few of the items that you will find at:

LadybugCertified.com

STEP 3 – MAKE A WREATH

First I recommend that you spend some time practicing your bow-making skills. Make them over and over again! That is the best way to learn. You can even use the same ribbon, and iron it if necessary in-between bows. The more you practice, the prettier your bows will be.

I would watch "Ribbons & Bows" over several times as you practice your bows. Please don't be discouraged if your first one doesn't turn out as you would like. But after several tries, you'll actually begin to see in your mind where each loop and streamer should be. That's the way it was for me. I did have a hard time with my first several bows.

Then, one day, something just clicked in my mind, and I thought: "WOW, I've Got It!! I can really see the bows as I am making the loops!" And, I did have it! I have been making beautiful bows ever since. And, my bow-making skills are still growing and changing to this day – as I'm sure yours will too.

I PROMISE THAT YOU CAN DO THIS!
I GUARANTEE YOU CAN DO THIS!

Next, you can start working on your wreath. Watch the wreath-making video once all the way through so you can become familiar with the terms, as well as my techniques, tips, and methods. Then you are ready to work along with my video.

Pause the video whenever you need me to stop so you can catch up. Rewind it when necessary. This IS NOT hard. It is SO enjoyable! As you get started, you'll be amazed at what you can accomplish with the correct instructions! Remember again... I know you can do it!

NOTE: Short-cut the process by working with me in person!
[http://passionintoprofits.com/workshop1/]

APPENDIX – HOW TO DECORATE A WREATH

STEP 1 - GET STEP BY STEP INSTRUCTIONS

STEP 2 – BUY SUPPLIES

STEP 3 – MAKE A WREATH

Now that you have learned how to make a wreath, you will want to start making wreaths as gifts and for special occasions. Not only will "you" want to start making more wreaths, but friends, neighbors, and even strangers will begin asking you to make wreaths for them. They will like the way your wreaths look so much, that they'll offer to hire you! This is when it is time to start expanding your wreath-making skills; as well as getting many of the questions that begin flying through your head, answered by me.

Beautiful Wreath Made in "Plantation Charm" e-Book

STEP 1 - GET STEP BY STEP INSTRUCTIONS

I have many videos to choose from which cover all seasons and different occasions. Some of these videos come in DVDs, and some are downloadable. More and more are being produced all of the time. These videos include wreath making, table arrangements, table Christmas trees, and tying beautiful bows.

(You can find my DVD selection here: LadybugCertified.com/store)
(You can find my Digital Video selection here:
http://ladybugwreaths.com/doorwreaths/download-videos/)

If you aren't sure which to choose next, then I would recommend trying "Welcome to My Garden"
[http://ladybugwreaths.com/doorwreaths/product/dvds/how-to-make-a-wreath-welcomegarden/]
or "Merry Christmas"
[http://ladybugwreaths.com/doorwreaths/product/dvds/christmas-door-wreath/]
depending on which season you want to focus on, and which style "strikes your fancy".

STEP 2 – BUY SUPPLIES & MATERIALS

You should have the basic supplies for making wreaths. (If not, you can review the list and purchase here.)
[http://ladybugwreaths.com/doorwreaths/product/wreath-making-supplies/]

You will definitely want to look over the supplies I use in my wreaths. Go to:
LadybugCertified.com to purchase the quality supplies that I use in my Ladybug Wreaths!

Here is where I do recommend watching the video all the way through at least one time (or more). Some of the wreath-making videos have bows, and some do not – just like some people like bows in their wreaths and some do not. So, decide if you need to purchase ribbon.

When I am purchasing supplies, I usually pick out my ribbon last. It will be much easier to match it to your flowers this way (or at least until you are a little more experienced).

You should buy your materials based on what you see me use in the video you are viewing.

First, you'll notice that I use a large mix of greens.

As you can see in the pictures above, I show you a large mix of greens as I discuss the many types and colors that look great in a wreath! And, I really like using at least three different types of greenery or more such as:

- Short grasses for tight or accent spots on the inside of your wreath. These are great to tuck in and around birds, nests, birdhouses, etc.
- Longer grasses which I use mostly from the outside of the wreath giving it a larger, wilder, and airier look.
- Ivy – I prefer mini leaf with long streamers so it can drape out from the wreath as well as wrapping around some of the honeysuckle vine and wild birch sticks radiating from your wreath.
- Then I always use leafy stems such as wisteria or ficus – and there are many more types of leafy stems. You can get GREAT prices on these if you have purchased "My Secret Vendor List". You can read about it here: "My Secret Vendors". [MySecretVendors.com]
- OR -- You can order the supplies I use here: **LadybugCertified.com**

The pictures above are clips from a video where I show you which flowers I am using. Take note of the types, sizes, and colors of flowers and berries used in the video you have purchased.

- If I am using two or three large flowers, then it will be easier for you to follow along with me if you have two or three large flowers.
- The same applies if I am using medium and small size flowers. Try to purchase stems as close to what I am using as you can. Choose colors that you would like to use.
- Pay special attention to see if I am using a flat flower like a Gerber daisy or a thicker, rounded flower like a hydrangea or a mum. Even this will make a difference when making a wreath for the first time. Later, you'll be able to make substitutions easily.
- And, I also use spiky flowers around the outside of my wreath to bring color out from the center. You can find these in many sizes and colors. Some are called Delphiniums, and then others may just be called flower spikes.
- If using fruit, pick out fruit which you would like to see in your wreath, and the same applies for stems of berries such as crab-apples, or just tiny berry stems.

STEP 3 – MAKE A WREATH

Now you can start making the wreath while you watch the video. Pause the video when you need me to slow down!

ALTERNATIVE – ATTEND A WORKSHOP

I have been asked countless times if I would teach in person. And, I have coached many women as time and health permitted through the years, but not nearly as much or as often as my customers have wanted. So, I will now begin running workshops in my home studio.

We will be offering a limited number of one-day intensive with just "you" and "me". My time will be your time for an entire day! I will teach you how to make any type of wreath that your heart desires!

Next, will be the one-day, Intensive small group workshop. There will be four or five ladies just like yourself. My assistant, Kim, and I will work one-on-one with each of you as we demonstrate how to make a beautiful wreath. You'll be making yours right along beside us!

Thirdly, is our Premium Intensive TWO day workshop which includes making a wreath as well as learning important business practices, Facebook Page setup, Etsy store setup. You will go home with a beautiful wreath for yourself or we can list it on Etsy, ready to sell! This workshop is designed to REALLY take your wreath-making skills as well as your business to the next level.

Each of these different coaching sessions include, your very own wreath supplies (wire cutters, glue gun, pipe cleaners, picks, floral tape, and green sheet moss), a custom designed "Ladybug Wreaths" easel and a beautiful, finished wreath.

If you are interested please fill out an application at: http://passionintoprofits.com/workshop1/

APPENDIX – HOW TO SELL YOUR WREATHS

Now that you have learned how to make different types of wreaths and have gotten positive feedback from family or friends, you may want to start making some money from your hobby.

Nancy started out years ago selling on eBay and had tremendous success there! It was a great start to her business. However over the years sales started slowing and she looked for other places to sell online.

After a lot of research, Nancy found that Etsy was the best place to sell your wreaths.

NOTE: If you have spent any time on the Internet, you have seen a lot of changes in the Internet and you need to shift your marketing strategies to maximize your online sales.

Etsy has become such a popular venue for handmade items (as well as vintage and other items) that is it not easy to get found and have a lot of sales.

The first step is to start selling on Etsy. You will want to set up your store and list several of your items. Next you need to send interested buyer to your store.

Next we recommend that you create a Facebook page and start building a list of fans who like your creations. This does take time but is a great way to get started.

After you have your Etsy store and a Facebook page, you will want to setup a Pinterest presence. This is a great place to interact with others and to build a following. You can create boards for your different creations.

How to sell online:

1. Etsy (your store)
2. Facebook (your audience)
3. Pinterest (exposure and audience)

BONUS – JUMPSTART YOUR BUSINESS

There is nothing like taking the 'fast track' to starting a business online. I made so many mistakes when I first got started but I plowed through the difficulties even though it took a lot of time and money. However, my income soared once I hired a coach--someone who took me by the hand and guided me through the pitfalls and eliminated my 'trial and errors.'

You can research and figure out how to do this over time. However, there is nothing like taking the 'fast track' to starting a business online. We made so many mistakes when we first got started but we plowed through the difficulties. Even though it took a lot of time and money, we have been able to make a great income.

However, our income soared once we hired a coach--someone who took us by the hand and guided us through the pitfalls and eliminated many 'trial and errors.' Although we are both hard and determined workers, never again will we waste time by trying to build our business without the guidance of a coach or mentor.

We offer two ways to 'jumpstart' your business:

1. Community/Training
2. Workshops

COMMUNITY/TRAINING

Best of Nancy Community (http://BestofNancy.com) – The purpose of this community is to have a place for members to interact and ask question as well as provide the training needed to start selling online.

There are two major benefits to being a part of this awesome group:

- o Forum - The favorite place to hang out for all the members is the forum.
    - You get to know each other and share successes
    - You can share difficulties and get advice and encouragement.
    - You can ask questions when you are stuck

    There are several sections in the forum:
    - Etsy – Member stores and how to use Etsy
    - Facebook – Member pages and how to use Facebook
    - Pinterest – Member Boards and how to use Pinterest
    - YouTube / Websites / Business Strategy/Planning
    - Making Wreaths
    - Boxing Wreaths
    - Shipping Wreaths

- Training – Video instructions on how to sell on the Internet using:
    - Etsy
    - Facebook
    - Pinterest
    - Website
    - Videos/Checklists/PDFs/Audios
    - Much, much more

WORKSHOPS

(http://passionintoprofits.com/workshop2/)

Our Premium Intensive TWO day workshop enables you to improve your wreath making skills as well as setup your business!

- o Day 1 – Nancy will work with you to take your wreath making skills to the next level! You will leave this portion of the training with a beautiful wreath!

  You have all of Nancy's supplies to choose from and you will receive your own wreath making supplies: wire cutters, glue gun, pipe cleaners, picks, floral tape, and green sheet moss.

- o Day 2 – Focus on starting your business. We will set up your Etsy store and show you how to create your first listing which will be one of the wreaths you just made in Nancy's shop. Nancy shows you how to take pictures.

  We will then setup you Facebook page and link your Etsy store to your Facebook page. You will learn about business practices, the best way to use social media to build your business and your next steps.

Your business is started when you leave!

Made in the USA
Middletown, DE
08 November 2015